Read The Manual

the little book
on how to write
for users
and
actually get read

by Peter Vogel

This edition published by PH&V Information Services,
53 St. Patrick Street, Goderich, Ontario, Canada, N7A 2L3

Edition: 10 9 8 7 6 5 4 3 2 1

ISBN: 978-0-9735355-1-8

Table of Contents

Introduction
or, Why I wrote this book

If you're like most people who create user manuals, job aids, or Help system content then the words 'technical writer' don't appear in your job description—but that's the job you're doing. And, if you're like most people who create user manuals (or any kind of end user documentation), you've probably also realized that:

- Your user manuals aren't read
- When people do read your user manuals they don't find the material helpful
- It takes far too long to create these documents that aren't read and aren't helpful when they are read

This book is here to help you with all three problems.

I want you to be a better and more productive technical writer. In writing user manuals, 'better and more' productive means two things:

- Your manual gets used more
- It takes you less time to create a manual

It's not your writing ability that's the problem. If you've successfully written a high-school essay then you have all the writing skills that you need to create a great user manual. So why aren't people using your user manuals?

There are three things standing in your way:

- Some of the things that you were taught in school don't work when you're writing a user manual.
- If you're like most people, you have a bunch of misconceptions about writing a user manual that prevent you from doing a good job.

- You're missing some of the tools that you need to do the work well.

This book will show you how to fix all of those problems.

A warning: If you are looking for the 'one right way' to create a user manual then you've come to the wrong place. The belief that there is 'one right way' to write a user manual, or a tutorial, or a job aid (or anything else, for that matter) is the single biggest misconception that leads to ineffective user manuals.

If there is no 'one right way', what will this book do for you? I'll show you three things:

- How to figure out what you should be doing
- How to write your material
- How to format your material

None of these three topics are complicated. And while I'll be talking about writing user manuals for software applications, much of what is in this book applies to any kind of technical writing…or for any document where you need to explain things to other people.

A final note: This is a self-published book. What does that mean to you? There are two costs and one benefit:

- The first cost is that this book doesn't have an index: my apologies. To compensate for that, I've kept the chapters short and put in lots of headings.
- The second cost is in copy editing (checking for typographical errors, spelling errors, etc.). I'm a terrible copy editor. If you find errors, let me know at peter.vogel@phvis.com and I'll fix them

What's the benefit to self-publishing? I didn't have to answer to anyone—I can write about what I've really learned in twenty-five years of doing technical writing/editing and teaching technical writing. This means, for instance, that I can tell you the truth about the rules of grammar that make your life miserable. It means that I can say things like 'a bunch of misconceptions' or 'like this' and not have my words changed to match some editor's arbitrary rule. You may not want to write for your users like I've written this book— but this isn't a user manual. This is me talking to you about how to write for users and actually get read—and, once you're being read, for your readers to know what you meant.

> **BTW:** These are my 'By The Way' boxes. It's material that you can safely skip. It's also material that I wanted to put in because I thought that the material was interesting (you may not agree). For instance:
>
> I stole the title for this book from one of the smartest people I know—Mike Kaplan (http://www.trigeminal.com/). He was going to use it for a book on how to read Microsoft documentation. Thanks, Mike!
>
> Looking back over the book, it's embarrassing how much I've stolen from Peter Dillon-Parkin, the technical editor for the writing course I wrote for Learning Tree International (http://www.learningtree.com /courses/319.htm). I also got to be technical editor on the business writing course he created. Thanks, Peter!
>
> The stuff that I didn't get from them I've taken from:
>
> - The fabulous editors (especially at the magazines) that I've written for
> - The instructors who teach my technical writing course and tell me what I've gotten wrong.
>
> If I start to mention any of them, I'll forget at least one, which wouldn't be fair. So: Thanks, all.

Why No One Reads Your User Manual

Or, You can't play darts with your eyes closed

Every time I teach the course on technical writing that I wrote for Learning Tree International © (www.learningtree.com), I get asked the same question: 'Why doesn't anyone read my stuff?' When people don't read your manual, you create costs—specifically for the help desk staff who must handle users calling up with questions answered in the manual.

The first thing you should know: You can't blame your readers. Studies have shown that over 90% of readers try to read the user

> **BTW:** 'RTFM' is an initialism, not an acronym—you have to be able to pronounce acronyms. So, FBI is an initialism, NASA is an acronym (I told you that these BTWs were material that you could safely skip).

manual. That only 30% persevere is your fault. Here's another great statistic: 70% would rather call the help desk then read the manual. Think about your last experience with calling a help line—exactly how awful was it? Yet people would rather do that than read what you write.

So why aren't your readers reading your user manual? The answer is simple:

> You're not writing about what your readers
> want to know.

I know that this sounds harsh but it's true. There was a wonderful study that analyzed several businesses over many years. The people doing the survey asked people if they got too much, too little, or just the right amount of end user documentation. The results:

Got too little:	50%
Got too much:	50%
Just right:	0%

Why? Because no one writing the documentation had bothered to find out what the readers actually wanted or needed. It's like playing darts with your eyes closed: half the time you'll be too high, half the time you'll be too low, and the odds that you'll hit the bulls-eye are zero.

There is one exception to this generalization: Some writers that don't get read are writing about what their readers want to read. In those cases, the reason the writers don't get read is either that (a) readers can't find the material they need or, (b) readers don't even know that the information is in the manual. This raises the eternal philosophical question, 'If the user's information falls in the manual and no one knows that it's there, does it matter?' The answer is 'No'.

Why Writers Fail

If you asked most authors of user manuals what was the first thing that they needed to research, they would tell you that they first have to learn about The Product. This is the second biggest misconception afflicting authors (the number one misconception is the belief that there is 'one right way').

In fact, the first thing that you must learn about is Your Audience. The reason that there is no 'one right way' is because every audience has different needs, different attitudes, and a different relationship to The Product. So every audience needs a different set of material.

Learning about your audience is not just a 'good thing to do'—it's a productivity issue. Authors who don't start by learning about their audience waste an enormous amount of time. Think about it:

- Are there features of The Product that your audience will never use? For instance, will your audience install The Product or will it be installed for them?
- Are there features of The Product that are known to your audience because it's just like every other product they use, so they already know how to use it (e.g. how to use the menu system, how to print)?
- Are there features of The Product that will only be used by advanced users who can figure it out for themselves?
- Are there features of The Product that will never be used by anyone?

If the answer to any of these questions is 'Yes' then why would you learn about those features? If your audience won't install The Product then you don't need to find out about the installation process. If, on the other hand, there are options that your audience needs that they must have installed then you must tell your audience to ask the person doing the installation for those features.

If you spend any time investigating topics that you won't write about then you're wasting your time. Furthermore, if you don't know your audience and what's important to them, you probably won't find out about what your audience actually does need to know. When you discover that you've missed a topic, you'll have to go back and revisit your research. It's the dart board problem again.

Authors who don't learn about their audience write too much. If you don't learn about your audience, you're going to write up everything that you know, that The Product's developer knows, or that anyone has ever known about The Product. You'll create a huge manual—the surest way to discourage readers.

If your manual is targeted towards your user, not only will you have less to learn and less to write about but you'll also create a smaller, better focused manual that will have a much better chance of being read.

Now, that's a productivity gain.

The First Thing To Do

The four most obvious things that you want to know about your audience are:

- What does your audience already know about the field (e.g. about working with computers)?
- What does your audience already know about products like The Product?
- What does your audience already know about The Product?
- How will your audience use The Product?

BTW: I sometimes have clients who object at this point in the process and say something like 'But what if there's one user who doesn't know how to <do something that most computer users know>?" I tell my clients three things:

First: I don't believe that user exists. You need to find that clueless user in order to prove to me that he or she is real.

Second: If that user does exist, how much do you want to spend to support one user?

Finally: How badly do you want to annoy every other user by creating a bloated manual in order to support that one user?

It's alright if you don't know the answers to these questions because, if you don't know, you can call up a couple of audience members and ask them (it's not cheating). I've been in a conference room with a writing team that spent two hours trying to decide if they needed to describe how to get to the Help system in a standard Windows product. The answer wasn't going to be found in that conference room no matter how long we argued about it. The answer could have been found in thirty minutes by calling up some audience members and asking them 'Do you know how to get to Help in a Windows application?'

Your first step in writing a user manual is to make up a set of questions that will let you find out what you need to know about your audience. For instance, you may want to know what the turnover among The Product's users is and whether or not the users work by themselves. If the turnover is low and users are typically surrounded by other users, you may not need to write a user manual at all—put on a training session, provide a quick reference sheet as a memory aid, and then let the users support each other. Here's a different scenario: Does The Product have a user interface that users find easy to use? Then skip writing the user manual.

> **BTW:** Think what *not* writing a user manual does to your productivity. Since productivity is output divided by time spent then, when time spent goes to 0, productivity becomes infinitely high. Beat that.

Every important question that you need answered about your user manual (including whether you need to write it at all) can be answered by referring to your understanding of the audience. And, if you can't answer a question by referring to your audience, it either means that:

- The question doesn't matter (your audience doesn't care)

OR

- You need to ask some more questions about your audience.

> **BTW:** There's actually a third choice but we'll get to that later. It only solves unimportant questions, anyway.

Handling Many Audiences

It's not unusual to find that you actually have several different audiences: beginners vs. experienced users; people doing data entry vs. people doing updates; people using one set of features of The Product vs. people using another set; and so on.

Installation instructions are a good example: It may be that you have two audiences: one is relatively inexperienced in the ways of software; the other is very experienced. The way that you will write the installation instructions for the first group ('Click Start and select All Programs...') will be very different from the way that you would write those instructions for the experienced group ('Run Setup.exe on the CD.'). Attempting to write a procedure to suit both audiences will succeed in turning off at least one of the audiences (and, potentially, both).

When you have different audiences then you'll need more than one user manual. Don't Panic! That doesn't mean that you have to produce several different books. What you do need is to segment the material. For instance, you could write up the material that the new users need, then the material that the software technicians need, then the material that the clerks in the shipping department need, and (finally) the material that the executives need. When it comes time to publish, you can bind it all together into one document.

For that single document to work, though, you need to do make sure that each section of the document clearly identifies who its intended audience is. You can do that in the table of contents or in the section headings (you can also, of course, bind the sections separately—installation instructions often seem to come in a separate book these days, for instance). In an on-line system, you could color code pages for different users.

> **BTW:** One of the benefits of binding the material for each audience separately is that each audience's manual is smaller. And (I'm repeating myself here), smaller user manuals are more likely to be read.

To have each section identify itself you must give it a title that reflects who will use the material. For instance, if executives only use the reporting functions, *don't* have the section on reporting functions called 'Reporting Functions'. Call the section 'For Executive Users.' If the clerks need some reporting functions, put the instructions for their reports in the section called 'For Clerks'. If there's some overlap between the two, you can either repeat the shared material in the Executive and Clerk sections or have a section labeled 'Reporting for Clerks and Executives.'

There are lots of benefits to this approach. Think about it this way: You're a clerk who has just opened a manual or surfed to the on-line Help system. You see a section called 'Reporting Functions.' Do you need to read that section? How would you know? If the section contains material on reports that you'll never use, how will you find the material that you do need? If, on the other hand, you are a clerk and, when you open the manual or Help System, you find a section labeled 'For Clerks' then that's a good clue that you need this material.

If you name your sections by the user's job or role then all you have to assume is that the reader can recognize their own job or role description. Of course, it's your responsibility, as an author, to make sure that the section contains the information that your reader needs and that you know the audience's job title (or role name).

There's one last audience to consider…

Readers vs. Audience: The Other Audience

I'm going to use the terms 'reader' and 'audience' almost interchangeably in this book but there is a difference between the two terms. The *audience* is the person that you're writing for; the *reader* is the person who is reading your manual. The worst possible situation for you is when your manual's reader isn't part of your audience.

I have a book on Amazon.com with fifteen 5-star reviews (and I only paid for one!). Why? Because the title of the book ('The Visual Basic 6 Object and Component Handbook') and the jacket copy made it very clear who should read my book. Do you want to attract a lot of 1 star reviews? Call your manual 'Everything that Anyone Would Ever Want to Know About The Product' and you have a title guaranteed to attract readers who aren't part of your audience.

The problem is that you *never* have just one audience. You're always dealing with at least two audiences: Your intended audience and the 'other' audience. The 'other' audience is made up of the readers that you don't want to read your manual. Your duty to the other audience is to prevent them from wasting their time reading your manual. You can do that in the title ('Microsoft Word for WordPerfect Users'), in the subtitle ('A guide for new users'), or the introduction ('This manual is aimed at experienced users.'). If you don't notify the other audience that this manual isn't for them, you'll only annoy them.

BTW: You can see the effect of not clearly identifying a book's audience by looking at the book reviews on Amazon.com. It's easy to find technical books that have both 1-star and 5-star reviews. The 1-star reviews say things like 'Too Simple' or 'Too Complex'. The 5-star reviews basically say 'Just Right'. The 1-star readers are from the 'other' audience and the author failed to keep them away from the book.

Your Reader's Scenarios

Or, There is no pipe and slippers

Once you know who your audience is you can go on to the second step: deciding what to write about. First an exercise: Right now, close your eyes and think about what your reader is doing at the moment when he or she is actually reading your user manual. Visualize your reader clearly before you carry on to the next paragraph.

What vision comes to mind when you thought about someone reading your manual? Did you picture a reader sitting at a desk, looking at page 1 of your manual? Is the chair tipped back or is the user leaning over the desk? What expression is on your reader's face? Did you picture your reader sitting in a comfortable chair, flipping through your manual? Is there a pipe and a pair of slippers involved?

The reality is that there is just one thing that about your reader that is almost certain: Your reader, at the moment that they reading your material, is *having a problem*.

No one reads a user manual for fun (if you do read user manuals for fun then you should recognize that you are *not* a typical audience member). In fact, users never read the material written for them unless they have to. Most people, when they get a new toy or tool just try to use the damn thing. They go to the manual only when things don't work out for them.

Do you doubt this? Think about yourself, then. You probably have a car and, if you do, your car probably has an owner's manual. Have you read it? Cover to cover? You might have completely read the user manual for your first car but, unless you're very unusual, you haven't read the manual that came with your subsequent cars (when I ask this question in class, about 10% of the audience has read their owner's manual cover-to-cover).

Like most people, you probably have read selected portions of your car's user manual. And which portions have you selected? My guess is that you've read the parts that you needed in order to handle some current problem: replacing a fuse, changing the time on the clock radio (twice a year), unlocking the hub caps to change a tire, checking to see what the recommended oil change schedule is, trying to figure out why those #$!# seatbelts won't move.

So, what does this tell you about your reader? Among other things, you can assume that your reader is:

- Already annoyed
- In a hurry
- Looking for an answer
- In the act of doing something (i.e. in the car wanting to leave for work)

There is no pipe and slippers. The chair is not tipped back.

> **BTW:** Yet another study (I love studies) showed that when readers find material that is actually useful to them, they will continue to use that material. Think about it: this means that if you give your audience what they want, they will keep reading your stuff.

What to Put In, What to Leave Out

The good news about this insight about your readers is that they care very much about what your user manual says—provided that your user manual talks about what your readers care about. To put it another way: Bad user manuals talk about The Product; great user manuals talk about the problem that the reader has right now.

> **BTW:** Knowing your audience and their scenarios has another benefit: it gives you a basis for prioritizing your work. Some audience members may never have problems; some audiences are so small that it doesn't make sense to support them; some audience members may have problems but would die before they would refer to the user manual. Ignore those audiences.

Now that you know your audience, you need to figure out what it is they will want to know. The better the job that you do of predicting your user's problems and needs, the better job you will do in giving your audience what they want. For any piece of information that you put in your user manual, you need to be able to answer one question:

> When would an audience member need this information?

You can only answer this question after doing a scenario analysis. It's your responsibility, once you know your audience and The Product, to figure out the scenarios that your users will follow when they work with The Product. Until you know what your audience's scenarios are, you have no idea what should or shouldn't go in your user manual.

A scenario has five parts (though one of the parts repeats):
- A goal: What the reader wants to do
- A trigger: What causes the reader to enter the scenario
- A series of tasks (the part that repeats)
- Feedback that lets the user know they're on track (or not)
- An end (when the user has achieved their goal)

If you don't know what the reader is trying to do (the goal), what starts the process (the trigger), the steps that make up the scenario (the tasks), what feedback they need, or what counts as the end of the job, how can you possibly write anything that will be valuable to your readers in their hour of need?

The User's Point of View

When looking at scenarios you need to take your audience's point of view. For instance, here are three examples of things that are NOT goals:

- Creating a new document
- Updating the SalesOrderHeader record
- Using the shortcut keys

Here are three examples of things that ARE goals:

- Creating a letter to mother
- Changing the ship date on a sales order
- Getting the job done faster to go home earlier

Goals are things that matter to your audience, not whatever drove the design of the application. For instance: No one has ever had, as one of their goals, 'to use a shortcut key'. However, some users are interested in 'getting things done faster' and may be interested in using a shortcut key as a means of achieving that goal. And, even in that case, your readers are probably only interested in getting faster at tasks they do frequently which means there are a limited number of shortcut keys they're interested in.

> **BTW:** I remember when user manuals came with a list of shortcut keys organized *not* by task but alphabetically by letter. It's as if the list author expected readers to wake up in the morning thinking 'Gee, I wonder what <ctrl_K> does?'

Looking at it another way: It's certainly true that, in order to achieve their goals, your readers will need to 'update the SalesOrderHeader record' but your *readers don't care about that.* Users care about 'creating a sales order.'

You need to also have the users' point of view of what counts as 'a task'. A user manual must use the same view of the world as the reader so that you can talk about the tasks that make up your reader's world. For instance, creating a sales order probably requires pulling information from several different sources (e.g. customer, product, and inventory information). Your reader might regard some of those retrievals as separate tasks and some as part of other tasks.

If you asked a user what they do in order to create a sales order, they might list just two tasks:

- Get the customer information (Customer record)
- Get the list of things the customer is buying (Inventory and product records)

> **BTW:** How do you find out what the tasks are from the users' point of view? Ask them! (it's still not cheating). Was a user requirements document created? Read it! Is there marketing material? What does that tell you about what matters to users?

You're not, in your user manual, obliged to support every possible scenario. There are only going to be a few scenarios where your user manual is actually going to be helpful. I wouldn't write about scenarios that:

- Are so obvious that no one in the audience will need help from you
- Happen so frequently that, in conjunction with some hands-on training, it's unlikely the reader will forget how to do it
- Happen infrequently but are so easy to remember that it's not worth spending the time to write about them
- Are only be performed by experts who will figure out how to do it on their own

Now that you know your reader's scenarios and which must be discussed, you can look at all the information that you have gathered about The Product and answer the key question from earlier in this chapter (rephrased):

> Under which scenarios that are worth writing about would an actual audience member use this information?

And that's all you need to write about. Don't start making up scenarios and audience members to justify some piece of information that you can't stand to leave out.

BTW: Often, when I explain that the user manual will support only some scenarios for some users, my clients object. They feel that we should support every scenario for every client (another misconception). In that scenario, I suggest that we put the additional information in the 'reference manual'. This document is cheap to create because it's organized arbitrarily (usually alphabetically), has brief descriptions, and has minimal formatting. And, better yet, it's usually dropped when deadlines are threatened.

Purpose

Or, The shortest chapter in the book

Your readers have a purpose in reading your user manual: They want to achieve the goals that you uncovered in the scenario analysis. You, too, have a purpose: What you want to do something *to* or *for* the reader.

For instance, when writing a user manual, you might have any of these purposes:

- Help new users get started
- Help experienced users become more productive
- Convince users the new system is actually useful
- Provide support for seldom performed tasks

Think of it this way: You're writing a book about how to determine how much income tax to pay. If you're working for the Canadian Revenue Agency (or the IRS or Inland Revenue) then your purpose is to help readers pay all the tax they owe; if you're a business management consultant then your purpose is to help readers pay the least amount of money they can (legally). It's not the same thing.

> **BTW:** I'm Canadian.

Your purpose forms the last part of the three things that you need to hold constant in your thoughts as you design and then write your document: your Audience, their Scenarios, and the document's Purpose.

Failing to consider any of these three points creates a document that doesn't meet the needs of anyone, doesn't help the audience with its problems, or has no point at all

Clarity

Or, Nobody knows what you're talking about

What does this piece of text mean to you:

> There are three theories to consider:
> - Labor-quantity theory (best shown by Smith's beaver-and-deer example)
> - Labor-difficulty theory (described by the famous reference to 'toil and trouble')
> - Cost theory (the theory used in most analyses)

My best guess is that this text is completely opaque to you (unless, of course, you have an understanding of economic theories of value—if that's the case then pretend that you just read something that you didn't understand).

How about this:

> I went down to the corner. When the light
> turned green (and the traffic stopped) I crossed
> to the other side.

Odds are that this text is transparent to you. Why? It's not because one sentence is written with shorter words or shorter sentences (the longest word in the first example is 'difficulty'). The problem with the first piece of text is that you don't know what the author is talking about. With the second piece of text, you know all about what the author is talking about.

Just because the second piece of text is transparent to you, it doesn't mean that it's transparent to all audiences. I can imagine someone raised in a remote community with no access to television, radio, or print and no understanding of living in a city.

What would 'corner' mean to that audience member? The corner of what? Their house? How about 'traffic'? Perhaps, the reader thinks, the author means 'business'? And, perhaps, this reader perseveres and reads further to the 'light turning green'. What could this mean to the reader? The sunlight turns green? And, finally, the reader gets to 'crosses over to the other side.' What was a prosaic story about city life has become a mystical experience about death.

You can't talk about anything unless your audience knows what you are talking about. Obviously, your manual has some new information to pass onto your audience. But you can't provide the new material unless you have ensured that your audience has been given enough background.

Where does that background come from? There are three possibilities:

- It's built into the language. No one has to do a study to determine that all bachelors are unmarried, adult, human males because that's what the word means.
- It's known to every member of the audience (i.e. if you're reading this book then you will know this). Anyone reading material about driving a car can be expected to know what a car is.
- You tell them (or tell your readers where to find the information).

You need to consider each piece of information in your manual and decide if it's going to be new to your reader. If so, you need to decide if the necessary background is in one of the first two categories listed above. If not, then you have to provide the necessary background information. You can either:

- Insert it into the text at that point
- Provide a reference to some other document (or some other part of this document)

Words

What does the word 'diction' mean? If you said 'enunciation' or 'pronunciation' then you're using a definition that has become increasingly common since about 1950. If you said, 'word choice' then you're using a definition that has become increasingly *un*common since about 1950. When I was going to school (circa 1956-1970), my teachers used 'diction' to mean 'enunciation.'

BTW: The site www.onelook.com lets you look up a word in several different dictionaries. I used it to look up 'diction' to get some idea of how the word has changed: The Webster dictionary of 1828 gives 'word choice' (or something like it) as the only definition. By the 10th edition (1993) of the Mirriam-Webster's dictionary, 'enunciation' appears as one meaning, but it's the third one. In the Encarta English Dictionary (1999), 'enunciation' appears as the first definition. Finally, the Cambridge Dictionary of American English (2001) gives 'enunciation' as the only definition. This is *not* an example of the language degrading, just of how the language is changing.

If you're going to write clearly then you're going to have to use each word with whatever meaning your readers have for that word.

Picking the appropriate vocabulary doesn't necessarily mean matching the vocabulary of your audience. Your vocabulary is going to be affected by your purpose. For a newsletter that I used to edit, our purpose was to provide knowledge coming from one programmer to other programmers. We wanted to sound like a very knowledgeable and trusted programmer, just like our readers. We also wanted to sound like we understood the problems that our readers faced. Our approach was 'geek-to-geek.'

On the other hand, one of the clients that I write documents for is a very large multi-national software company. My client wants their material to sound like the authoritative voice on their software. My client wants readers to believe that the information that is provided in their documentation is beyond reproach. They want their material to be not just read, not just understood, but *believed*.

These two different purposes result in two different vocabulary choices. For Smart Access, I used contractions, words from common speech, and referred to the reader as 'you' and the author as 'I'. For my client, I don't use contractions, I stick to words that appear in official documents, and the author seldom appears in the documents.

If you're worried about clarity (and you should be): Make sure that your readers know what you're talking about and that you're using words they actually know with the meaning they actually use.

BTW: While new words do appear and words change their meaning over time ('silly' once meant 'saintly') you do have to use the words that actually exist. On an episode of Good Morning America I saw displayed on the screen the message that you should keep 'your mortgage in tact.' There is no place or thing called 'tact' that you can keep things in. Things that you want to keep in one piece are kept 'intact.'

Poor Words

In addition to using words with the meaning that your readers have for that word, you also want to pick words with as few meanings as possible. The more meanings that a word has, the more likely it is that a reader will pick the wrong one. So, rather than pick words that are 'rich' in meaning, you want to pick works that are 'poor' in meaning.

Often picking the word with the fewest meanings also means being more specific—another good way to improve clarity. The unintentional humour that comes from newspaper headline like 'Police Shoot Man With Knife' comes from using a word that has many meanings (in this case, the word 'with'). On the other hand, using a more specific word with fewer meanings eliminates the problems: 'Police Shoot Man Holding Knife.'

Grammar

Or, Why your English teacher ~~lied~~ misled you

I'm going to take this chapter and the next to talk about the lowest level of 'how you should write it': grammar and punctuation. What I'm not going to do is give you a lesson in grammar—if you can speak the English language you already know everything that you need to know about grammar. I also know that you had n number of years of English classes that attempted to teach you the rules of grammar; I know that many major newspapers have a column from some 'language maven' moaning about how bad everyone's grammar is. I also know that those English classes and those mavens are misleading you (see the BTW that's coming up).

At this point you know who your reader is, what scenarios they will use your information in, and what your purpose is. You can use that information to make decisions about how you should write your information, including decisions about grammar and punctuation.

Grammar and punctuation may sound like an area where you don't have to worry about your readers. There are, after all, rules for correct and incorrect grammar, aren't there? And if there are rules then it doesn't matter who your reader are, does it? Don't you just follow the rules?

No, you don't.

You should also realize that there are a number of rules that you were given in school that you shouldn't follow when writing a user manual. Many of the rules that you were given in school were designed for creative or academic writing. The idea that grammar is immutable and universal is another of those misconceptions that prevent you from writing effectively.

Grammatical Errors

Is it possible to make mistakes in grammar? Sure. You can say things like this:

> The textbox are highlighted in blue.

But, let's face it, you'll spot this kind of mistake as soon as you re-read your work. This is a 'one-off' mistake caused when (a) your mind drifted off, or (b) you revised the sentence and missed some parts, or (c) your fingers just got tangled in the keyboard. This is not the kind of mistake that you're worried about.

What you are worried about are things that you do wrong all the time and don't even know are wrong: 'systemic' mistakes. You're not sure what those mistakes are but you probably wonder about when to use 'who' or 'whom', 'It is I' or 'It is me', 'The data is…' or 'The data are…'.

And people do make systemic mistakes. I watch Good Morning America, a show that would be unable to fill its two hours of airtime if some small child wasn't imperiled every day in somewhere in the United States at least once in the week. One segment was about a small boy who had been caught under a grand piano. The show's hosts were interviewing the police officer who had pulled the boy from under the piano. Had the officer been interviewed while saving the boy, he would have said that 'I'm dragging the boy from under the piano.' Since the boy had been saved the day before, the officer said that 'I drug the boy from under the piano.' Is 'drug' wrong? Should he have said 'dragged'?

You don't care. If that officer is part of your audience and says 'drug' should you write 'drug'? The short answer is 'Yes.' If that bothers you, though, I have good news for you. While the police office *says* 'drug', he probably *writes* 'dragged.' So, in writing material for users, you need to pick the appropriate *written* grammar. Don't worry about your grammar—find out about your audience's grammar. There are a couple of studies that show obsessing about grammar interferes with your ability to write well.

> **BTW:** The rule that gives the past tense for 'drag' as 'drug' is the same rule that gives the past tense of the word 'sing' as 'sung.' Many words that used to follow this rule in English, no longer do. For instance, in English, the past tense of 'work' used to be 'wrought' (which still survives in 'wrought iron'). Over time, in English, irregular verbs like 'sing' and 'work' become regular verbs and, so, 'drug' becomes 'dragged.'

As an example, do your readers say 'The data *is* stored...' or 'The data *are* stored...'? My guess (and I'm willing to be wrong about this) is that your readers say 'The data *is* stored...'. The grammatical police who insist on 'The data *are* stored...' justify their decision by referring to the etymology of the word 'data': The word has Greek roots where the plural is indicated with an 'a' at the end (the singular is datum). Since 'data' is a plural, the correct version of the sentence is 'The data *are* stored...' You don't care: Your readers say 'data *is*' so you write 'data *is*.'

It is, of course, possible to have grammatical errors. And, in fact, eliminating them is critical to achieving credibility with your readers because readers tend to overreact to grammatical and spelling errors. When readers see grammatical or spelling errors they tend to react as you do when you see a cockroach in a hotel room: readers assume that your document is infested with errors.

However, because you have researched your audience and are using their grammar you aren't making any systemic errors. You may, though, have some 'one-off' errors embedded in your manual. To prevent the cockroach problem (and maintain your credibility) your last pass through your document should be to find and eliminate those one-off errors. They're easy to spot (especially if you have someone else do it, as I do) and easy to fix.

BTW: You've never heard of Bishop Lowth but he's the main reason that you suffered taking grammar back in school. Let me begin by asking you a question: When did the first English grammar book appear? I've got a timeline below that marks out the centuries with the names of some famous English authors from that period. I've started in 1400 because that's when the version of English that we use first started to appear:

1400	Geoffrey Chaucer
1500	Sir Phillip Sidney (he was famous at the time)
1600	William Shakespeare
1700	John Dryden
1800	Charles Dickens
1900	Agatha Christie

In what century did the first English grammar appear? The answer is: the 1700s—and the late 1700s, at that. So for almost four hundred years people were speaking English without the benefit of anyone telling them how to do it. And, given the state of public education, for the next two hundred years the vast majority of people probably continued to speak the English language without anyone telling them how to do it.

So, I ask you, how could anyone possibly tell all of these people that they were speaking English *wrong*? Bishop Lowth could.

In 1780, Bishop Lowth published a grammar book that explained how Shakespeare, Milton, Dryden (and the common rabble like us) had been using English incorrectly. The problem Lowth decided, was that we weren't speaking Latin.

Lowth assumed that languages degenerated over time. Obviously, then, earlier languages (like Latin) were closer to being 'right' than more modern languages (e.g. the English of 1780). So Bishop Lowth invented rules for English based on the way that completely different languages worked.

For instance, Bishop Lowth noted that you can't split an infinitive in Latin: in Latin you can say 'to go boldly' but not 'to boldly go'. Why? In Latin, the infinitive ('to go') is one word. Lowth decided that if couldn't split infinitives in Latin, then you shouldn't split infinitives in English, either.

The bishop also applied logic to the English language: The words 'shall' and 'will' were used interchangeably by English speakers. Since it made no sense (to Lowth) to have two words that meant the same thing, he invented a distinction between the two words. Since 1780, English teachers have been trying to enforce that distinction and English speakers been ignoring it. The main result is that people avoid using 'shall' because they're afraid they'll get it wrong.

Audience Matters

As I've suggested, the etymology of 'data' is fascinating but irrelevant when deciding grammatical issue. Even though the word 'silly' originally meant 'saintly,' if you tried to use 'silly' to mean 'saintly' you wouldn't meet either your readers' goals or your own (and references to the word's etymology wouldn't solve the problem). In current English, for most readers, 'data' is singular. Any attempt to use 'data' as a plural noun will just sound odd to most of audiences. If readers think you've made one mistake, they'll think you've made lots of mistakes (it's the cockroach problem again).

Do notice the modifier in my previous paragraph: 'for *most* readers'. If your readers are an academic audience where most readers have a doctorate in computer science, I would seriously consider using 'The data *are* stored…'.

BTW: I've run into the grammar police on many occasions. For one of my books, I had a copy editor who felt that sentences shouldn't end in a preposition (this is another Lowth rule: it's impossible in Latin). I had written a bunch of sentences like this:

> This is the point that workflow has arrived at.

The copy editor rewrote those sentences to:

> This is point to which workflow has arrived.

I sounded like a pompous ass. Winston Churchill once remarked, satirically, that a preposition at the end of a sentence was 'something up with which I will not put.'

Here's the final point that I want to make in the area of grammatical errors: Pick your battles. Everyone has an area of expertise and, when it comes to grammar, everyone is an expert. Your work will almost certainly be reviewed by managers, peers, and others. People who wouldn't dream of correcting your technical knowledge and wouldn't try to write anything longer than an e-mail message will leap at the change to apply some obscure rule of grammar that they've carried with them since public school. Unless you think that it's going to make a difference to your readers or your purpose, just implement their changes and move on.

At this point someone reading this book is thinking 'There are rules, you know' or 'If you let people break the rules the language will degenerate.' First, protecting the language is not your problem; helping your reader is. More importantly, no one wrote a specification for the English language—people just made it up as they went along. People are still just making it up as they go along. It's a good thing: You wouldn't want to speak like Shakespeare, Samuel Johnson, or Charles Dickens.

Having said all that, there are a few areas related to grammar where you've probably been led astray: pronouns, synonyms, and modifiers. I've picked these topics because, as an editor, these are the grammar-related areas where I have to do the most work to ensure clarity. And it's not just my opinion that most writers need some guidance in these areas. One study showed that these three items were among the major contributors to confusion in readers.

Pronouns in Action

A pronoun is a short word that stands in place of a longer word. For instance, in these two sentences 'it' stands in for 'textbox':

> On the right-hand side of the screen is the textbox for the user's name. When the form is first displayed, it is highlighted in red.

The problem with this sentence is that the reader doesn't know that the 'it' in the second sentence is a stand-in for the longer word 'textbox' in the previous sentence. I gave you that information before I showed you the sentence but your reader won't have that advantage—the reader only has the words on the page, not the words in the writer's mind.

Look at my sample sentence from the reader's point of view: When readers get to the word 'it', they have to figure out what the word 'it' stands for. How many candidates are there for this job? At a bare minimum, the reader has a choice between five possible candidates:

- The subject of the sentence that the word 'it' appears in: 'The form'
- The last noun in the previous sentence: 'The user's name'
- The subject of the last sentence: 'the textbox'
- The first noun phrase at the start of the previous sentence: 'the right-hand side of the screen'
- The subject of the noun phrase at the start of the previous sentence: 'the screen'

Of these five candidates, how is the reader to pick out the right one?

> **BTW:** Technically, this problem is called 'ambiguous pronoun antecedence'.

The only possible way for the reader to figure out the right answer is to replace the pronoun with the various candidates until they get a sentence that makes sense:

- When the form is first displayed, *the form* is highlighted in red.
- When the form is first displayed, *the user's name* is highlighted in red.
- When the form is first displayed, *the textbox* is highlighted in red.
- When the form is first displayed, *the right-hand side of the screen* is highlighted in red.
- When the form is first displayed, *the screen* is highlighted in red.

Presumably, some candidates are never considered and 'more likely' candidates are considered first (the order that I have above seems like a likely search order). It might be an interesting academic study to try to determine how readers resolve this kind of ambiguity. But that's missing the point! You don't want to make your reader's search more efficient—you want to eliminate the search altogether.

The real point is that are three problems here:
- You're wasting the reader's time processing candidates
- The reader will recognize that they have to make a mental pause to do that processing and accuse you of being 'hard to read'
- The reader may pick the wrong candidate.

As an example of 'picking the wrong candidate', think about what happens if the reader picks my second example as the appropriate decoding for the word 'it' ('When the form is first displayed, *the user's name* is highlighted in red.'). You may now have planted in the reader's mind that the form will appear with the user's name already filled in. At the very least, the reader is going to run into problems when, later in the document, you describe how to enter the user name ('Hold it,' the reader thinks, 'isn't the name already entered?').

The solution to the problem is simple: never use pronouns. Rewriting the previous sample sentence to follow the rule gives this result:

> On the right-hand side of the screen is the textbox for the user's name. When the form is first displayed, the textbox is highlighted in red.

By explicitly referring to the textbox the reader is saved some mental processing and you avoid having the reader make the wrong choice.

There are two objections to my blanket condemnation of pronouns:
- You'll end up repeating the same words over and over again.
- The text will be too wordy

Both objections are ill-founded. In creative writing, repeating the same words over and over again may well be a bad practice: the sound of the word begins to grate on the ear. In a user manual, you're less concerned with the sound of the sentence than with ensuring that the sentence's meaning is unambiguously conveyed to the reader: Repetition in the defense of clarity is no vice. In addition, remember that a manual isn't read like a book. It's unlikely that a reader will read enough of your document to make the repetition a problem.

People who worry about the text being 'too wordy' were told that they must be 'concise'. As far as the text becoming too wordy, the number of words in both versions of my sample sentence is the same (though 'textbox' is longer than 'it'). The sentences are equally 'wordy.' More importantly, with the original sentence the reader has to substitute 'textbox' for 'it' in their mind to make sense of the sentence. By doing that replacement for them, you reduce the mental processing required by the reader. And reducing demands on the reader is, presumably, the point of being concise.

> **BTW:** My 'no pronoun' rule is probably too strict. I'm sure that you'll find that I do use pronouns in this book, if you look carefully enough. The rule that I really use might be stated as 'No pronouns unless I have a gun to my head.' When I do use a pronoun it almost always refers to the immediately preceding noun. And I never use pronouns to refer to abstract concepts.

Synonyms

If pronouns are evil, synonyms are eviler (years from now, 'eviler' will be a word: you read it here first). With pronouns when a reader hits a word like 'it' they know that it's a stand-in for another word and look for the replacement. With synonyms the reader may not be aware that there are two different words that are referring to the same thing.

> **BTW:** The first user manual that I ever wrote was about a sales order system. In that book I had seven different names for one screen. To this day, I'm not sure if my readers thought there was one screen with seven different names or seven different screens that looked *very much alike*. What can I say? I was young, I was foolish, I needed the money.

Try this sentence:

> An XML document provides a structure for data. Each XML instance consists of tags and text. The markup provides the structure for the data.

Did you know that 'document' and 'instance' are synonyms? How about 'tags' and 'markup'? Or 'text' and 'data'? What are the chances that someone unfamiliar with the information will figure it out?

A simple rewrite that uses the same word for the same thing (e.g. just 'document') eliminates the problem:

> An XML document provides a structure for data. Each XML document consists of tags and data. The tags provide the structure for the data.

Modifiers

A modifier is a word or a phrase that modifies the meaning of something else. The most typical examples of modifiers are adjectives (which modify nouns: the *green* house) and adverbs (which modify verbs: the *fast* horse). Clauses also act as modifiers (the box *which is on the shelf*).

Most modifiers used by most writers are, most of the time, useless. Those writers are still responding to what they were told in high school: 'Make your writing evocative and descriptive'. In a user manual clarity matters, not 'being evocative'.

> **BTW:** Did you wince when you read 'most typical'? Grammar mavens will tell you that things are either 'typical' or not (these are the same people that will say that the phrase 'a little bit pregnant' doesn't make sense). They're wrong. In English, words like 'most' and 'more' are intensifiers, not logical terms. If you disagree, you'll have to argue with Thomas Jefferson who wrote about creating a 'more perfect union'. And you'll also have to argue with any number of women who knew they were 'a little bit pregnant' at some point in their life.

There are three tests that you should apply to any modifier before letting it remain in your document:
- In this situation would anyone every say the opposite?
- What—if anything— is lost if the modifier is omitted?
- Can you rewrite the sentence to turn the modifier into a verb or a noun?

As an example, look at this sentence:

We welcome your *valuable* input.

Would anyone ever say 'We value your *useless* input'? If not, adding the modifier 'valuable' is unnecessary. If the modifier is deleted, you have 'We value your input'—from the reader's point of view, has any information been lost? Finally, the sentence can be rewritten to give 'We value your input' which both eliminates the modifier and makes the sentence shorter.

Being Concise

You may have wondered if I was ever going to talk about being concise (you may also have noticed that I have trouble being concise). For many authors, being concise is an end in itself. Quite frankly, I think that being concise is overrated. I would rather simply not talk about a topic than worry about talking about it concisely; if I do talk about a topic, I want to make sure that I meet all of the readers' goals.

Also, as the section on modifiers demonstrates, concision falls out of doing the right things. If you do what's best for your reader then you'll end up with text that's as concise as it needs to be.

I do have one bit of advice that does relate to concision: eliminate meta-talk. Meta-talk occurs whenever you comment on your own writing. This sentence is an example of meta-talk:

> In this section we'll discuss the impact of water

Instead of talking about what the section discusses, the writer could just have provided an effective title for the section. If an introduction of some kind is required, it could be

> This section discusses the impact of water

Or just

> The impact of water is…

Sentence Variety

Making concision an end in itself encourages writers to use a lot of simple sentences, which makes reading their documents like being sent a series of Twitter tweets. What readers actually value is a variety of sentence structures: simple, compound, complex, and compound-complex. Any good grammar book will show you how to create all of these. When I'm editing, I normally find too many simple sentences rather than too few.

My advice? First, don't worry about achieving concision by using short words: Use the words that your readers know. Second, while simpler sentence structures should appear most, don't avoid the longer sentence styles. Think of your paragraphs as a series of clauses that you can join together to form sentences in any combination you want. For instance, that previous sentence could be written in any of at least three ways:

> Think of your paragraphs as a series of clauses. You can join those clauses together to create sentences. You can join these clauses in any combination you want.

> Think of your paragraphs as a series of clauses. You can join those clauses together into sentences in any combination you want.

> Think of your paragraphs as a series of clauses you can join together. You can join those clauses into sentences in any combination that you want.

I like the last version. However, you'll notice that after that very long sentence, I began this paragraph with a very short sentence. It's the variety your readers will appreciate (another short sentence).

Punctuation

Or, The language is as she is *spoke*.

People who want to specify grammar can, at least, fall back on the way that English is used by native speakers. Presumably, a group of native speakers can be selected and then a set of rules that describe the way that those speakers use the language can be created.

But what about punctuation? No one speaks punctuation. As a result, all rules about punctuation are purely creations of printers and writers ('writers' in the sense of 'people who put words on paper'). Punctuation is purely a matter of convention with no possible recourse to authority other than tradition.

BTW: I love reading interviews where the person being interviewed uses parentheses in their response:

Interviewer: When did that happen?

Interviewee: While I was at school (1967, as I remember).

How, exactly, did the interviewee say those parentheses? The comedian Victor Borge had a hilarious routine where he pronounced all of his punctuation. The practice has not been adopted.

Thinking About ?,.;!

A recent movie had the title 'Two Weeks Notice' and a number of grammar mavens felt that the title should have included an apostrophe: 'Two Week's Notice'. The grammar mavens accounted for the *ess* sound at the end of 'weeks' by insisting that the *ess* was being added to indicate possession.

The rationale for insisting that the *ess* indicates possession is that people would also say 'One month's notice.' Since, in that sentence, 'month' is singular mavens insist that the only reason for the *ess* sound is to indicate possession. Therefore, the mavens claim, the *ess* sound at the end of 'two weeks' is also indicating possessive and should be punctuated 'week's'. This approach makes sense only because the question assumes the answer.

I can make a case that the appropriate analogy for '*two weeks* notice' is 'the *red* house' or 'the *green* ball'. In other words, 'two weeks' is a modifier (an adjective), not a possessive noun. If so, the *ess* sound at the end of 'two weeks' doesn't require an apostrophe because it indicates plurality. I would imagine a conversation that goes like this:

She's given us notice.
How much notice?
She gave us two weeks.
So, she gave us the two weeks notice.

However, people do say 'one months notice' and we are obliged to account for the *ess* sound at the end of 'month'. I would prefer to justify the plural in the spoken sentence as an example of back-formation. Back-formation occurs when speakers, over time, convert one structure into another because the structures look (or sound) similar. Back-formation is what, over time, converted the original French 'a numpire' into the English 'an umpire' and converted the original 'an ekename' into 'a nickname (and 'Clumb' into 'Climbed'). I can claim that most people gave notice in multiples (four days, two weeks) rather than in singulars (one week, one month). Since most notices were multiples, as a result of back-formation, all notices have become plural.

Your goal is not to arbitrate language issues; your goal is to avoid the cockroach problem. The right answer is to ask some members of your audience to write down any disputed phrase and use the punctuation that your audience uses.

Changing Styles

Here's my point: Most discussions of punctuation assume that the rules of punctuation are immutable. Nothing could be further from the truth. Punctuation varies from one editor to another and from one age to another. And not just in details, either.

From a historical point of view, punctuation is diminishing in importance. The world is moving towards an open style of punctuation where fewer punctuation marks are used. Presumably, this reflects that modern (more literate) readers need less guidance than earlier readers. This is good news for you: The fewer punctuation marks in use, the less chance that you'll get something wrong.

BTW: It's easy to show the change in punctuation style over time I compared two works published around 1800 (a poem called 'The Task' by Cowper and 'The Idler' by Samuel Johnson) and two works published around 1950 (a poem by Dylan Thomas and an essay by I.F. Stone).

Cowper has 13 punctuation marks in his first 50 words (1 semi-colon, 1 dash, 2 periods, 7 commas, and 2 apostrophes): a ratio of words-to-marks of 26%. The Dylan Thomas poem had 10 punctuation marks in the first 80 words: a ratio of 13%. Samuel Johnson's first paragraph had 12 punctuation marks in the first 80 words (8 commas, 2 semi-colons, and 2 periods): a ratio of15%. The I.F. Stone essay had just 3 marks in its first 80 words: a ratio of 4%.

For instance, it used to be a common practice to mark the introductory part of a sentence with a comma (like the comma after 'For instance' at the start of this sentence). With the move to a more open style of punctuation, these commas are disappearing. The assumption by the printers, editors, and authors involved is that modern readers don't need the comma to recognize that an introductory phrase is not part of the main sentence.

To be fair, not everyone has followed this trend. Some editors still insist on a close punctuation style that includes the comma following a phrase at the start of a sentence (me, obviously).

If you think that you only need to follow the rules, consider that many sentences can be punctuated a variety of ways, all of them 'correct':

> With modifications the storage management system supports up to 200 drives in series without any degradation in performance.

> With modifications, the storage management system supports up to 200 drives in series without any degradation in performance.

> With modifications the storage management system supports up to 200 drives in series, without any degradation in performance.

> With modifications the storage management system supports up to 200 drives in series— without any degradation in performance.

> With modifications the storage management system supports up to 200 drives (in series) without any degradation in performance.

> With modifications the storage management system supports up to 200 drives, in series, without any degradation in performance.

How do you decide which set of punctuation to choose?

Instead of applying rules for the sake of applying rules, why not find a way to apply punctuation that helps the reader? Don't worry about 'right' and 'wrong' when writing a sentence. Instead, take an *operational* view of punctuation. An operational view treats punctuation marks as a toolbox that you draw on in order to solve problems. Think first of what message that you want to send to your reader. Then pick the punctuation mark that will do the job for you.

Colons and Lists

An operational approach to punctuation probably reflects the way that you currently use punctuation. When you want to start a list what tool in your punctuation toolbox do you reach for? A colon.

A colon is a flexible tool. You can use it to introduce both:
- Bulleted lists
- Lists inside a sentence (in-line lists)

There are alternatives to using a colon. You can mark the start of a list with words: 'these examples illustrate', 'By following these instructions', 'as shown below', or even with a just 'like these.' However, every one of these alternatives involves more words than just using a colon and doesn't accomplish any more than the colon does. In fact, each of these phrases will have a colon at the end, anyway.

When do you use a bulleted list versus an in-line list? From an operational point of view, it depends on where you want to put the emphasis: on the list as a whole or on each individual item? A bulleted list emphasizes the items on the list. It's hard to ignore individual list items when each has a line to itself. An in-line list emphasizes the list itself because all of the list items are part of the same sentence. Within a sentence, you can even eliminate the colon, de-emphasizing the list as a whole by merging the list with the sentence.

The Serial Comma

An in-line list needs commas to separate the items of the list: apples, peaches, and pears. This raises the contentious issue of the *serial comma* (in England, the *Oxford comma*). This is the comma that precedes the 'and' in a list of more than two items. Do you use the comma:

Apples, peaches, and pears

Or do you omit the comma:

Apples, peaches and pears

First, you're asking the wrong question. The first question that you need to ask is 'Why are you worrying about this?' Outside of an Oxford don, do you think that any of your readers care? Your readers will certainly value that you be consistent, so pick one of the two options and carry on.

Serial comma fans (me) point out that the serial comma can be used to mark joint terms that appear as a single item in the list. This example that omits the serial comma:

We had tea, bread and butter and tarts.

Without the serial comma it's hard for the reader to see that 'bread and butter' is a single unit in the list. But let's be realistic: the number of times that this problem appears is very small. As fond as I am of the serial comma, in most situations a simple rewrite lets you omit the serial comma:

We had bread and butter, tea and tarts.

> **BTW:** Another solution is to use a bulleted list (though this may give too much weight to the items on the list).
>
> We had:
> - Bread and butter
> - Tea
> - Tarts

Hierarchies of Information

Inside a sentence, an operational point of view allows you to see punctuation as a way to establish levels of emphasis within a sentence, as a hierarchy of information.

Think of it this way: a normal sentence has a single level of importance. Putting part of the sentence inside commas, like this, reduces the importance of that that part of the sentence. Material inside of parentheses (like this) is lowered even further. On the other hand, dashes—like these—raise the enclosed part of the sentence to a higher level of importance.

Joining Sentences

While you can use 'and', 'or', 'but' to join sentences together, you can also join sentences together with punctuation marks:

> Think of your paragraphs as a series of clauses
> that you can join together; you can form clauses
> into sentences in any combination that you
> want.

There are two punctuation marks that you can use to join sentences: semi-colons and colons. If you have two clauses that you want to bring together into a single sentence but want to maintain some distance between them then use a semi-colon; it's that simple. If you have two sentences that you want to bring together where the second sentence represents a conclusion drawn from the first then the answer is plain: Use a colon.

The End

To mark the end of your sentence you use a period (in England, a full stop), a question mark, or an exclamation mark. Your default choice is the period. If you want your reader to treat the statement as a question, use a question mark. If you want your reader to be surprised or to otherwise remark on your sentence, use an exclamation mark. However, the more that you use exclamation marks, the less impact that they will have.

> **BTW:** When I'm working as an editor, I tell authors that they get one exclamation mark per article: Use it wisely.

This isn't everything that you can do with punctuation but it's most of what you need.

The Importance of the Style Guide

Or, It's just like real estate

If there are no rules for many areas (grammar, punctuation), what do you do? The old joke in real estate is that the three most important criteria for a house are:

1. Location
2. Location
3. Location

For your reader, the three most important criteria are:

1. Consistency
2. Consistency
3. Consistency

To put it another way: Readers don't care whether you type one space or two after the period (quick: which rule do I use? Do you care?). Readers do care if you keep changing the number of spaces.

This means that you can divide all questions into two categories:

- Things your readers care about
- Things where consistency matters

For the first category, you can get the right answer by asking some members of your audience (it's not cheating). For the second category, you need to make an arbitrary decision. For both categories, you need a style guide to record these decisions in.

What falls into the 'arbitrary decision' category? At the very least, these items:

- Capitalization: Do you want to use an 'up' style which capitalizes all the important words (e.g. 'I am the System

Manager') or a 'down' style which capitalizes only proper nouns (e.g. 'I am the system manager')

- Numbers: Switching between digits (1, 2, 3) and words (one, two, three). One company I worked for used words for any number that needed, at most, two words (e.g. 'one hundred') and digits for the rest (e.g. 101)
- Names of things: What is your company's name? Is it 'Fred' or 'Fred, Inc.'?

For any of the 'arbitrary decision' category items, there is no right or wrong and it's not the intent of your style guide say what's right. The intent of the style guide is to ensure that you (and the rest of your team) are consistent over time.

There is another benefit to having a style guide: You only have to make these arbitrary decisions once. Without a style guide, you will have to endure endless discussions and challenges about every punctuation mark.

Good news: You don't have to create a style guide from scratch ; 'The Handbook of Technical Writing' by Alred, Brusaw, and Oliu is a good choice for your first style guide. For technical writers, the style guides aimed at journalists are probably more useful than ones aimed at academics (e.g. the 'The Associated Press Guide to Punctuation'). Industry-specific guides also exist (Sun, IBM, and Microsoft have all published style guides, for instance) so look for one for your industry.

Bad news: Having just one style guide isn't going to be enough. As my list suggests you'll probably need a guide for grammar/punctuation issues, a dictionary to determine spelling, a guide for industry terms, and another for company-specific terms. One warning: For any particular topic (grammar, punctuation, etc.) have only one style guide. If you have two guides for any topic, your guides will disagree with each other.

You may have wondered about why I've devoted so much space to grammar and punctuation so early in this book. The reason is that you don't want to write your document and then make up your style guide. If you do, you'll have to go back and revise the document to be compliant with your guide: A process that's boring, tedious, and error prone. You need to build your style guide before you start writing and after you've determined your audience, scenario, and purpose.

> **BTW:** While I recommend style guides aimed at journalists, for sheer authoritative weight, it's hard to beat 'The Chicago Manual of Style.' It's both a literal and metaphorical weapon (the book is *huge*).

Solving Problems

Every important problem that you face in writing a user manual can be resolved by asking the question "What's the right answer according to our audience, their scenarios, and our purpose?" All the unimportant problems can be resolved by asking the question "What does our style guide say?"

Organizing Your Material

Or, Nothing goes in by default

If you skipped ahead to read this chapter first because this is the area you have the most problems with—forget it. You need to go back and read the chapters on audience, scenario, and purpose first. You can't organize until you've completed the steps described in those chapters. Why? *Because there is no right way to organize your material.* Your document's organization must reflect the reader's needs, the reader's vocabulary, the reader's problems, the reader's view of the world. You don't live in a vacuum and neither does your user manual.

Generate, Then Organize

The first step in organizing your material is to generate all the topics that you could possibly want to talk about. For this step only, *don't* think about your user. Instead, concentrate on generating without criticism or editing all the possible topics that you can think of. Discard nothing.

Once you have the topics, the second step is to start organizing them. Now you can go back to thinking about your audience and their scenarios.

Task vs. Internals Organization

Why think about your readers' scenarios? Because the organization that you apply must reflect a *task-based* structure. The tasks that you use are the ones from the audience's scenarios.

The opposite of a task-oriented structure is an internals-oriented structure. It's easy to spot an internals-oriented structure when looking at the table of contents for a Help system or manual. A document with an internals-orientation will have a table of content whose titles will reflect any one of:

- The structure of the programs
- The menu structure of the application
- The tables in the database
- The division of jobs among the programming team

I've seen all of these. None are useful to the reader.

Some internal-oriented structures can be mistaken for task-oriented structures. Organizing topics according to the menu structure of the application is one of these. But think for a minute about how the reader will find information that they need. Does anyone come into work thinking 'Gee, I need to know what the second item on the Tools menu does?' The answer is 'No.' That's because picking the second item on the Tools menu is not a task to any user.

The truth of the matter is that a typical task often begins before the user starts the application. Once in the application, the user frequently uses several different forms or menu choices to complete the task. If something goes wrong with the task, the user often has to fix the problem by going to a completely different part of the application. No menu oriented structure will bring these sequences of steps together into a coherent whole.

One bank's help desk discovered that 60% of all questions could be answered by reading the appropriate section out of the manual. You could assume one of three things:

1. Users are lazy/stupid
2. Users enjoy calling the help line
3. The manual prevented users from finding the information they needed

Remember that:

- You are a user and you're not stupid
- No one likes to call the help line

Assuming those two items, option 3 sounds like the most likely choice as to why users weren't taking advantage of the manual.

It turned out that the manual was organized into two major sections: Customer functions and Credit Functions. This structure reflected the way that the teams that built the system had been organized. However, to add a customer (a typical task), users had to use functions from both areas. Because of this mismatch between the tasks and the manual's structure no one bothered to try to use the manual. Instead, they called the help desk which found that 60% of all questions...

The bank recognized the problem and reorganized the manual around things that their users actually did: Add A Customer, Update A Customer, Review Customer Credit History. Users actually started to read the manual and the number of help desk calls dropped.

> **BTW:** Another non-useful organization method is a forms-based structure. The plan is take a screenshot of every form in an application and then describe every field, button, checkbox, etc. on the screen. What people like about this plan is that it's easy to tell when you're done.
>
> The result is useless to readers. First, any particular task usually requires users to move through multiple forms. Second, for any task, only a small number of the widgets on any form are required. Worse yet, this methodology gives equal importance to widgets that are used all the time as it does to widgets that are hardly (if ever) used.

Organize and Prune WITH

As you generate and organize your material, you'll almost certainly learn several things about the topics that you generated:

- Some groups of topics will be missing topics
- Some topics don't belong in any groups
- Some topics are really the group headings for other topics

Learning these things is not a bad thing. It doesn't mean that you did a bad job of generating topics.

The first item on the list is actually an important part of the process—it's unlikely that your brainstorming will have turned up all of the topics that you should cover. The organizing process helps you identify those gaps.

Also, don't be afraid to have topics that don't belong in any group: It's OK to have single topic chapters (go back and look at the Purpose chapter in this book). Don't force-fit a topic into a chapter just to avoid a single topic chapter.

The final stage of organizing your material is to delete material that your readers don't need. The mantra that I chant while I'm doing this is WITH: Why Is This, Here. The part before the comma is most important: 'Why Is This'?

The question 'Why Is This' is answered when the answer to *all* of the following questions is 'Yes':
- Is there some scenario that you're supporting where your audience member would use this information?
- Would a reader need to look up this information?
- Does this topic support your purpose?

No topic item should make it into the material unless it can justify itself against all three questions—nothing goes in by default.

Now that you've organized and pruned your topic list you should take one last pass at the structure of the topics. This uses the full WITH: Why Is This, *Here*. You know why the topic is in the material, now you need to be clear why it's at this place in your structure rather than somewhere else. Again, these decisions should reflect your audience's view of the material, driven by their scenarios and your purpose.

Some topics may need to be in two places. You have two solutions:
- Put the topic in one place and put a reference in the other place (e.g. "see 'Adding a New Customer'")
- Repeat the material

The first choice is best. Repeating the material not only increases the size of your manual and increases the amount of work that you have to do, it almost always ensures that the two pieces of material will eventually contradict each other (old saying: 'A man with two watches never knows what time it is.').

The Final Pass

You're now ready to make the final, critical study of your document's structure. For each topic that you intend to write, ask yourself this question:

> After reading this topic, how will my reader use
> The Product differently?

Often, the answer is 'Nothing.' If so, you can eliminate the topic.

Are you, for instance, including:

- A history of The Product
- A history of the technology
- Acknowledgements to all the wonderful people who helped you
- Descriptions of how your product works

This is all wonderful material that you are passionately interested in—your reader could not (repeat: no matter how much they tried, your readers could **not**) care less.

If reading a topic will not result in a measurable change in the actual behavior of your readers—if reading your material will not make your audience *do something differently*—then why are you including this material? If you can't make a difference in how your readers' will use The Product, leave it out.

Providing Information

Or, What to write

Once you start to write your topics, you need to consider what kind of information your reader wants/needs.

What to Present

There are four kinds of information that readers need in a user manual:

- Concept: When the reader needs to be introduced to the The Product; When the question being asked is 'What is X?'
- Overview: When the reader needs to be told what the The Product consists of; When the question is 'What are the components of X?'
- Task: When thc reader needs detailed information about achieving their goals with The Product; When the question is 'What about X matters to me?'
- Procedure: When the reader needs to know how to accomplish some task with The Product; When the question is 'How do I do this with X?'

Don't feel obliged to use all four categories when writing. Many technical writers find that the distinction between Overview and Task information is of no help to them.

If you've ever tried to use online Help and wondered 'What are they talking about?' what you've probably been missing are the first three levels of information. While the online Help provides all the procedural information a reader needs, it's often missing the concepts and background that would let the you understand the procedural information.

Having said that, omitting concept/overview/task information is not necessarily a bad thing. If you can count on your readers knowing about the topic then including that information is (a) a waste of their time, (b) a waste of your time, and (c) only going to create a bigger document that fewer people will read.

> **BTW:** Many times, I've had clients who have insisted on including concept information where there is no reason to believe that a reader would need the information. When I've pressed to omit the information, the result has often been to just reduce the amount of concept material to the point where it would be of no use to anyone who didn't already know it. Not only did we waste my time in writing material that no reader needed, we wasted my time in producing so little material that anyone who actually needed it wouldn't be helped—and probably insulted the actual readers who must have felt 'Do they think I don't know this stuff?' If no reader needs it, the correct answer is not to do 'a little of it'; the correct answer is to do none of it.

Order of Presentation

The overall structure of any part of your document is 'When—Key What—More What.' The start of the section must tell the reader when this information is applicable. You can supply the When through a heading or title ('Word for WordPerfect Users': only WordPerfect users using Word need to read this), with the first sentence of the section ('The overall structure of any part': only readers interested in structure need to read this), or the first words in the sentence ('You can supply the When': Only those interested in how to apply When information need to read this).

If the reader continues past the When then it's your responsibility to supply any essential information first: What the reader needs to know to achieve their goals. Only after supplying the essential information do you supply any additional information.

It's often tempting to provide 'critical' rather than 'essential' information first. Critical information includes specific problems to avoid, information on handling unusual cases, tips to improve performance—single pieces of information that prevent disaster or help the reader to do things better. However, what the reader wants first is the information that allows them to achieve their goals and, only after that, include information about unusual cases or potential problems.

> **BTW:** Another point about the distinction between 'essential' and 'critical' information—readers tend to assume that the amount of space devoted to any topic reflects the information's importance. The information that is essential to helping the reader achieve their goals should, therefore, occupy more space than other information, no matter how critical. If you find that the information necessary to handle, for instance, a special case that doesn't occur very often is taking more space than handling the typical case then you should consider moving the special case to an appendix.

How to Present the Information

Once you've determined what kind of information your reader needs, you can consider how you're going to provide it. There are probably an infinite number of ways of presenting information but you can get by with seven. In general, those seven ways can be classified according to what kind of information you are providing.

For introducing a reader to The Product (Concept) you can use any of three methods:

- General-to-Specific: Begin with an overview of the topic and then drill down to specific examples. This is the most useful method when the reader is completely unfamiliar with the material.
- Specific-to-General: Start with specific examples (ones relevant to the reader) and move up to the background. This is the best choice when there are some examples that are relevant/known to the reader.
- Compare-and-Contrast: Start with information that the reader is familiar with and show how the new information is similar to or different from that information. This is especially useful when the reader has a 'large enough' body of knowledge in one area that can be used as a springboard into a new area.

Where you need to provide the reader with information about the components of The Product (Overview), there are two methods that work well:

- Order of importance: Start with what's most important to the reader and finish with what's least important. This method allows the reader to stop reading when you get to material that has low value to the reader. Newspaper stories are frequently written in this fashion with all the important information in the first paragraph and increasingly less important information towards the end.
- Effect-and-Cause: Start by describing what the reader can get (or has got) and then describe what's necessary to get it (or get out of it). This format describes the product to the reader in terms of what the product will do for (or to) the reader (the effect). Error message manuals are usually written in this style: You've got this error message (the effect) and here's why you've got the message (the cause).

When you give readers information they need achiving their goals with The Product (Task), Effect-and-Cause also works well.

However, if there are several ways that readers' could achieve their goals you should use:

- Problem-Methods-Results: Describe the problem or goal the reader faces, describe the various mechanisms for achieving that goal/resolving the problem, and provide a mechanism (the Result) that the reader can use to decide which method to use (e.g. 'this method is fastest but more expensive').

Often, when the reader is given several different ways to do something, the writer omits the 'results', leaving the reader wondering which method they should use. Using Problem-Methods-Result ensures that you provide the reader with a means for choosing the method that's best for them. If the benefits of any method can be brought out without discussing any other method, you can include the result in the description of the method. However, if you need to compare the different methods then you should defer the result until you've discussed all of the methods and then use Compare-and-Contrast to give your readers a way to select the method that's best for them.

Finally, when it comes to providing a step-by-step guide to performing some task (Procedural), you can't do better than:

- Narrative: Do this, then do this, then do this, etc.

One warning: Don't take this assignment of 'ways of presenting information' to 'types of information' too seriously. For instance, compare-and-contrast is an excellent tool for presenting information at all levels except, perhaps, Narrative. Overview and Task are so closely related that any method that works for one will work for the other.

Tutorials

A special form of narrative is the tutorial. Many authors of user manuals treat tutorials as a kind of training material. The scenario that they imagine is users working through the tutorials in the manual, executing each one in order.

That's not how readers use tutorials.

Here's how readers really do use tutorials:

- When readers need some procedural information that will help them achieve one of their goals, they flip through the manual until they find a tutorial that shows how to do what they want
- Readers then work through the tutorial, skipping any steps they think are unnecessary and modifying the remaining steps to meet their goals
- Readers often don't get to the end of the tutorial. Instead readers abandon the tutorial part way through when they feel they've "got it" or when the readers' goals diverge from the tutorials steps.

If you think about it, this is probably the way that you use tutorials, too. Guess what: In this respect you're like your readers.

Tutorials are not training tools—they're empowerment tools. When using a tutorial, users are not 'readers,' they are 'do-ers.'

Since that's the way that readers use tutorials, you have to write your tutorials to support your readers. To begin with, the tutorial must begin with a task-oriented title or introduction that allows readers to find the tutorial they need. Most steps in a tutorial will have three parts:

- The first part describe what the step does so that readers can decide if they need the step and how they can modify the step to meet their goal
- The second part of the step must tell the reader what to do
- The last part of the step provides feedback so that readers can determine if they've done the step correctly

Here's a bad tutorial. Among other problems it's too abstract (it doesn't solve any problem), is intended to demonstrate some technology rather than meet a reader's goal, doesn't tell the reader what's being done in each step, and provides no feedback:

Disk Caching Speed Up
1. Start any wizard
2. Click the start button

3. Click Next. Click Next. Notice how long each page takes to display
4. From the Tools | Options dialog check Disk Caching
5. Etc.

A useful tutorial is oriented around some task that the user wants to perform and uses the three part format for most steps:

Displaying a Table on the Internet
1. To start the Wizard that creates your page, select the Web Page Wizard. The first page of the Wizard displays.
2. Select the table that you want to display from the dropdown list at the bottom of the page.
3. Give your page a name by entering a valid name in the Table Name text box.
4. To select the fields you want to display, click the Next button. The Select Fields page displays.
5. Select the fields you want to display by checking those fields in the list.

Handling Errors

One last note: Think back to the last time you used a tutorial. Did you get it right the first time? Probably not. Again, this is one of the few places where you are like your audience.

To deal with this problem, your first step is to test your tutorial: Find a typical member of your audience and watch that person work through your tutorial. As your 'typical user' makes mistakes or has problems, your first step is to recognize that the problem lies with your tutorial and not with your user. Your second step is to deal with the problems that your 'typical user' has uncovered.

The obvious solution is to rewrite any steps that the user stumbled over, typically by making the steps longer. This is the appropriate solution if the instruction isn't clear or if you feel the step will be misunderstood by a large percentage of your readers.

However, rewriting the instruction isn't always the best solution—by making the step longer you are, effectively, punishing all of your readers because one reader had a problem. You also need to recognize that, often, there is nothing wrong with the instruction the user stumbled over. In many occasions, the reader just misread the instruction. If you think about the problems you had with your last tutorial many of them wouldn't be fixed by rewriting the instruction: you just made a mistake.

A better solution is insert a problem/resolution step after a step where some users may have a problem A problem/resolution step has two parts:

- Describe the problem. Readers that don't have the problem can move onto the next step in the tutorial
- Instructions on how to solve the problem for those readers that do have the problem

Using my previous example, a revised version of step 3 would look like this:

3. Give your page a name by entering a valid name in the Table Name text box
   Problem: *I get a message that my table can't be created.* Make sure that you haven't used any punctuation marks in the name that you've entered.

Creating Sentences

Or, How to write it

Now that you've selected the topics that your reader is interested in, organized them according to the readers' scenarios, decided what kind of information the reader needs on each topic and how you'll present it, you're ready to start writing the paragraphs and sentences that make up your manual. And you'll do all that while following the style guide you've developed. With all of those constraints in place one of two things will happen: What you need to say is so obvious that the sentences will practically write themselves...or you'll lock up completely as you try to meet all of these demands simultaneously.

Relax. You can't do it so don't even try—at least the first time.

The Power of the Rewrite

Assume that you'll start off writing something terrible, something that's wrong because it doesn't address the document's audience/scenario/purpose, uses the wrong vocabulary, introduces material that the reader isn't prepared for...there must be a thousand ways that you can fail. So take it for granted. You can fix your failure when you rewrite.

You should assume that your initial writing effort will just provide the raw material that you'll use during your rewrites. That initial effort will take about 25% of your total writing time while the remaining 75% of your time will be spent in rewriting that material.

> **BTW:** I remember the first piece I wrote for publication. I had put it off until two days before the deadline and now had to write something (I had signed a contract and, besides, they were going to pay me). I typed in the first sentence, looked at it, and thought 'Well, that's about the stupidest thing anyone's ever written.' After a couple of rewrites the sentence moved to the middle of the article and, as I remember, disappeared completely in the third revision.

Rewriting is not about fixing mistakes; Rewriting is about adding excellence. Every rewrite makes the document better. You don't stop rewriting a document because it's perfect. Instead, you stop because:

- You're out of time ('It's not done, it's due')
- Your time would be better spent on another task
- You're completely sick of the document and will throw up if you have to spend one more minute on it

Writing the Great Sentence

A great sentence in a user manual begins by telling the reader what it's about and then delivers on that promise. It delivers on that promise by clearly identifying what the sentence is discussing, providing information that the reader values, and by not putting up barriers to readability.

Your first goal is to make sure that the sentence is about what the reader is interested in. If the reader is interested in some *thing* then that *thing* should be the subject of the sentence; if the reader is interested in the *action* then that *action* should be the sentence's primary verb.

This approach to structuring sentences will, occasionally, generate a sentence written in the passive voice. You will, occasionally, bump into an editor who has been told that the passive voice is bad. Ignore them.

BTW: A sentence written in the active voice has a subject that performs the action; a sentence written in the passive voice has a subject that is not performing the action. For instance, this sentence is in the active voice because the subject ('the boy') is performing the action ('hit '):

> The boy hit the ball.

This sentence is in the passive voice because the subject ('the ball') is not performing the action:

> The ball was hit by the boy.

In general, sentences in the active voice are shorter than sentences in the passive voice. Editors who obsess about being concise often favour the active voice.

For instance, this perfectly good sentence is in the passive voice:

> A dialog box appears.

You could rewrite it to convert it to the active voice:

> The application displays a dialog box.

You'd be wrong: The reader is interested in the dialog box not the application and, at the expense of introducing another topic into the sentence ('the application'), you have moved the focus from what matters to the reader ('the dialog box'). Focus your sentence on what's important to the reader for the topic currently being discussed and everything will work out.

Use Parallel Structures

The chapters on grammar and punctuation covered much of what you can do to eliminate barriers to readability. However, those chapters were mostly concerned with what you shouldn't do (e.g. *don't* use pronouns, synonyms, modifiers, or nothing but simple sentences). There are some positive things you can do to improve readability, though.

If you're using a variety of sentence structures then you'll have compound and complex sentences. You can help your reader out by using a parallel construction for each phrase in these sentences. For instance, this sentence uses a different structure for each phrase:

> After opening the furnace door, the fire grate
> should be lowered.

This sentence, however, uses the same structure for the second phrase that was used for the first phrase (verb-noun):

> After opening the furnace door, lower the fire
> grate.

Alternatively, you could use the same structure for the first phrase as was used in the second phrase (noun-verb):

> The furnace door must be opened before the fire
> grate is lowered.

Remember that your reader doesn't have access to the words in your mind—your reader has only the words on the page. To alert your reader that you are using parallel construction, repeat the words at the start of each phrase. This sentence doesn't repeat any words so the parallel structure isn't obvious to the reader:

> You can create a new document by using the
> File menu or pressing <ctrl_N>.

This sentence makes the parallel structure more obvious by repeating the word 'by':

> You can create a new document by using the
> File menu or by pressing <ctrl_N>.

Creating Cohesion

Repeating key terms has a more general use in creating cohesion in your document. For instance, this example discusses programming objects in Microsoft .NET. Unfortunately, each sentence sounds like it's starting a new topic:

> Defining objects in .NET can be done in a number of different ways. The Entity Framework and LINQ-to-SQL designers will create objects for you. Class files, written in any .NET-compatible language, allow you to create objects.

Repeating key words both eliminates synonyms and tells the reader that you're still taking about the same thing (remember: readers only have the words on the page). This version of the previous example repeats a keyword from near the end of the previous sentence at the start the next sentence.

> Creating objects in .NET can be done in two *ways*. One *way* is to let the designers that come with the Entity Framework or LINQ-to-SQL *create your objects*. You can also *create your objects* by writing code in any .NET-compatible language in a Class file.

Another strategy is to use a set of key words at the start of a section and repeat those key words near the start of each related section:

> *Defining objects* can be done in a number of different ways. You can *define objects* using the Entity Framework or LINQ-to-SQL designers. You can also *define objects* by writing code in a Class file using any .NET-compatible language.

A third variation on this strategy is, at the start of the section, to announce the words for the topics that you intend to talk about and then repeat those words when you're ready to start discussing each topic:

You can create objects in .NET in two ways: use *the built-in designers* or *write code in Class files. The built-in designers* include the ones that come with the Entity Framework or LINQ-to-SQL. W*riting code in Class files* lets you use any .NET-compatible language.

Writing Headings, List, and Columns

When writing headings your goal is to support the reader finding the section they want. Your first goal, therefore, is to structure your headings around the users' scenarios. You also want to move the key terms towards the front of the heading.

The following table of contents begins every topic with the same four words. Readers have to go to the fifth word in each heading to determine if the chapter is the one they want:

How to calculate employee base pay
How to calculate employee vacation pay
How to calculate employee overtime pay

This version moves the unique part of each chapter title to the start:

Base pay calculations for employees
Vacation pay calculations for employees
Overtime pay calculations for employees

These same rules apply to the column and row headers in tables and lists: the headers should reflect the questions that the reader asks and the distinctive part of each header should be at the front.

A table with headers like this makes it difficult for readers to determine what each column or row describes:

	Calculating Deductions for Pension	Calculating Deductions for Health Plan
Employee Base Pay		
Employee Vacation Pay		
Employee Overtime Pay		

This version of the table moves the distinctive part of each heading to the front. The repeated part of each header moves to the table's title:

Calculating Deductions on Employee Pay

	Pension	Health Plan
Base Pay		
Vacation Pay		
Overtime Pay		

The same strategy works well for lists by moving the common part of each item to the introduction for the list:

To calculate employee:
- o Base pay, see page 20
- o Vacation pay, see page 24
- o Overtime pay, see page 28

Formatting the Page

Or, Making your page think

To understand how important formatting is you need to think about how your audience will carry out the physical act of reading your manual—what are the actual actions that your readers will perform? Perform this mental experiment: Close your eyes and imagine watching someone reading a novel. Now imagine someone reading a newspaper.

If you have a strong visual sense, you will have recognized that people read different kinds of documents differently. People read novels by starting at page 1 and moving sequentially through the pages. People read the newspaper by skimming the front page of some section (not necessarily the first section—I start with the entertainment section) looking for interesting stories, then flipping to the second or third page, skimming that page, and so on.

Now imagine this: you, the last time that you used a manual. I imagine that it looked something like this:

1. You searched the table of contents for the problem that you were having
2. If you found something that looked promising you flipped to that part of the book
3. If nothing looked promising, you used the index to find a promising part of the book and then flipped to that part of the book
4. You then started scanning the manual looking for a heading about your problem or for a picture that looked like what you were doing

5. When you found something that looked like your problem, you skimmed the text to get the general gist of what was being discussed

6. Only if the section had what you wanted did you actually start to read that section

Guess what? That's the way everyone is trying to read *your* manual. The least that you can do is write your manual to make that part of the job (searching, scanning, skimming) work for your readers.

Studies have shown that readers scan the page first and break the page down into sections. Readers then prioritize the sections that they've found. Finally, the reader reads the sections in the order that they've prioritized the sections. Notice that it isn't until this last step that the reader actually reads your words. Your page format must support this process by having a structure that reflects the reader's interests.

You've already done much of this work. You've written your manual around the user's scenarios. You've broken out the topics of interest to your readers. All in all, you've done a heck of a job of supporting your reader's scenarios. Now your page format must show that work. Your page must think for your reader in order to free up your reader's time to think about their problems.

Your goal is to create blocks of text (and graphics) that represent the structure of your document. Breaking your page up into blocks supports the first part of the reader's page processing process. The reader sees the blocks of texts as the items that need to be prioritized.

To simplify this discussion, I'm going to ignore graphics (pictures, diagrams, screenshots, etc.) and just talk about working with your document's text. For this discussion, a block consists of a heading that describes the contents of the block, followed by one or more paragraphs.

Tools of the Trade

Don't panic. You don't need to become a graphic designer in order to create effective page designs. For instance, you need only two tools to create your blocks: whitespace and alignment. Items that share the same alignment and are surrounded by whitespace appear as a block.

So, to create a block you must do just two things:

- Put more whitespace around the block than inside it
- Have all of the block's components share the same alignment

In other words, this set
of words looks like a block.

This set of words

does not look like a block

What's the difference? The first block has more whitespace around it than inside it; both sentences in the block are aligned along their left-hand edge. The second (non-)block has as much space between the lines as is around the block; the two sentences do not share an alignment.

BTW: Centering text guarantees that the sentences in your block will share no alignments. These two sentences, for instance, are centered:

This is the first sentence in my block
This is the second sentence

Centered text looks like a series of lines, not a block. Centering should be avoided except for single lines that stand apart from everything around them.

To create a block, begin by aligning the block's components along some side. Because English readers read right-to-left, a left alignment is best. Full justification, which gives a smooth border on both sides of the paragraph is ideal but often creates unfortunate gaps in the middle of the paragraph. Aligning the left hand side of the block and leaving the right-hand side ragged is the easiest to manage (and what I've used in this book).

> **BTW:** Here's an example of the unfortunate gap that can occur in centred text:
>
> Visual Studio is a great environment   for creating .NET programs by automating common   tasks and catching errors.
>
> Where gaps line up, as you can see starting to happen in this example, they're referred to as 'rivers.'

You also want to have more space around your blocks than inside of them. Each block should begin with a heading, so you want to have more space *before* each heading than between the heading and the first paragraph in the block. You also want to have more space before and after the block than between the paragraphs that make up the block.

You also need to mark the beginning of each paragraph. This can

> **BTW:** Many formats separate headings from the text that the headings belong to (presumably, to make the headings stand out). This separates the heading from the text and breaks up the block. The result is that, when the reader scans the page, they see a bunch of single line blocks (the headings) unattached from any text.

be done two ways:

- Indent the first line of the paragraph
- Insert extra space between paragraphs

If you choose to indent the first line of your paragraph there's no need to indent the first paragraph after the block's heading. In fact, indenting the first paragraph breaks up the union between the heading and the body's alignment.

This layout uses an indented first paragraph:

This is a heading
    This is the start of the first paragraph of the
block. This is the second sentence

The result looks less like a block than this layout which omits the indent:

This is a heading
This is the start of the first paragraph of the
block. This is the second sentence of

If you mark the beginning of each paragraph by putting space between paragraphs then you need to have more space between blocks than in between paragraphs.

How much space do you need between blocks? The answer is relative: The amount of space between blocks is relative to the amount of space inside the blocks. Since I've put space between paragraphs, I need more space between blocks than I have between paragraphs. In order for the human eye to spot the difference in size, the difference between space inside the block must be at least 33% greater than the space inside the block.

In this book, to create the space between paragraphs, each paragraph is followed by 5 additional points of empty space: this is the space between paragraphs. To create additional space between blocks, each heading is preceded by 6 points of empty space. As a result, where a paragraph ends a block, the combination of the 5 points after a paragraph and the 6 points before a heading creates an 11 point gap between blocks: over twice the difference between paragraphs.

Fonts and Headings

Now you need to provide a way for your readers prioritize the blocks. The headings for your blocks provide the best way of helping readers prioritize the blocks. This creates conflicting priorities: You want your headings stand out so that your readers can find them but you also want your headings to look like part of the block that they introduce.

Whitespace and alignment will make the heading and paragraphs look like parts of the same block. To make your headings stand out you just need to use two fonts: one font for your headings and a second font for the body of your block. They key is to make sure that the two fonts are as different as possible.

Fonts differ on the basis of three characteristics:

- Serif or non-serif. Serifs are those little wingies at the ends of the lines that make up a letter.
  This is a letter in a serif style: M
  Here's the same letter in a san-serif style: M
  In the serif m you can see the serifs at the top and bottom of the vertical lines.
- Variation in line thickness. Some fonts have great variation and others do not. In the serif M the thickness of the two vertical lines differ (as does the thickness of the two slanted lines). The san-serif M has no variation in the lines.
- The stress of the letters. Stress only exists in letters that have variation in line thickness. To measure the stress of a font, draw a line through the thinnest parts of the letter o in the font; the greater the slope of the line, the more stress the font is said to have. This letter has no stress because a line drawn through the thinnest portions of the line is vertical:

O

Begin by picking a font for your paragraphs. Research tends to show that, on paper, readers find serif fonts easier to read so you should use a serif for your body text. Serif fonts generally have variation in line width and some stress. So your headings, to be as different as possible, should use a san-serif font with no variation and no stress (or a stress in the opposite direction from the body text).

In this book, I've used Times New Roman (serif, variation, some stress) for the body text and Arial (sans-serif, no variation, no stress) for the headings.

Text can also differ in posture (bold, italics) and size. In this book, I've put headings in bold and left the text plain (where I've wanted to use posture to emphasize text inside my body, I've used italics).

For size, you must make text at least 33% larger for the human eye to see the difference. In this book, the paragraphs are in 12 point (about as small as my 55-year old eyes can read comfortably) so I've made the section headings 16 points (33% larger than the paragraphs). The chapter headings are 22 points (33% larger than the section headings).

> **BTW:** There doesn't seem to be any useful research on the best font size for your body text. What is known is that readers read groups of words and find it easier to read lines that contain between 10 and 15 words. Fewer words in a line and reading speed slows down; More words and readers have to read the line in two groups. In this book, the size of the page and my font size (12 points), gives a word count of roughly 13 words per line.

One final point: Since your headings are what your readers use to find the material they want in your manual, your heading font needs to be easily readable. Stay away from the decorative fonts (e.g. *Freestyle Script*).

> **BTW:** A decorative font is any font that would give you a headache if you read it for more than 30 minutes.

In addition, you want to avoid using block capital letters or underlining in your headings. People don't read words by parsing them out 'letter-by-letter.' Instead, for each word, readers look at the first letter, the last letter, and the word's overall shape. The overall shape of the word is controlled primarily by its ascenders (letters that stick up above other letters like *l* and *d*) and descenders (letters that extend down below the line like *g* and *q*). Using capital letters or underlining hides the shape of the word.

Headings in Margins

I've been assuming that you're going to put your headings above the text that it introduces, as I've done in this book. If you've chosen to have a large empty margin to the left or right of the text and place your headings in the margin, alignment still matters. The simplest solution is to have the top of the first paragraph align with the top of the heading.

In the following example, the bottom of the heading line aligns with the bottom of the first line in its block (notice that I've still made the heading as different as possible from the paragraphs to make the headings easy to spot):

This is the second last paragraph in the preceding block in the column.

This is the last paragraph in the preceding block in the column. This is its last line.

The Heading

This is the first paragraph in the block with the heading to the left. The bottom line of the heading aligns with the bottom of the first sentence.

This is the second paragraph in the block with a heading to the left.

You still need to make sure that the space after the end of the block is greater (by at least 33%) than the space between the paragraphs that make up the block. In the example above, I have 5 points between paragraphs and 11 points after the last paragraph in the block.

Columns

Research has shown that lines with more than 15 words (or less than 10) are harder to read. If your paper size and chosen font size will give you a line longer than 15 words, you have two choices:

- Use wider margins. Research has shown that the more empty space there is on the page, the less intimidating readers think that the material is. If you make one margin much larger than the other (i.e. a wide left-hand margin) you can put graphics, icons, or interesting material (like my BTW boxes) in that area.
- Use a two column design. This assumes that you will have at least 10 words per line in each column with sufficient space between the columns that readers won't find the lines from the two columns running together. This may also

create a more crowded page that will look more intimidating to readers.

BTW: If you want to reduce the number of words in a line, you can, of course, increase your font size—but only at the expense of increasing the size of your manual. If want to increase the number of words on a line (and the size of your manual), you can reduce your font size—but only at the expense of legibility. As our population ages, you should consider 12 point fonts as the minimum legible size. If your readers are younger than 40, you can consider 10 point or even an 8 point font (though I think 8 point is too small even for younger readers).

Lists and Tables

Headings aren't the only tool that you have at your disposal in helping your readers prioritize blocks. Formatting lists clearly helps readers spot them on the page. Typical list structures include:

- Using bullets for each item on the list (which also helps distinguish between list items when the items span more than one line)

  Indenting list items from the rest of the block.

7. Numbering items, which helps flag to readers that this list is a set of steps to perform.

In this book, I indented my lists from the left and used a ragged right alignment. The result is that my lists share no alignment with the rest of the block its part of. This creates a danger that my lists will appear as separate blocks on the page, separate from the heading or the paragraph that introduces the list.

Since alignment was no help, my solution was to use the other tool to create a single block of a paragraph and a list: whitespace. I needed to handle three scenarios:

- For the list itself to appear as a block, I made sure there is less space between list items than there is between blocks
- For the list to appear as part of the block that includes its introductory paragraph, I made sure there is less space between the last line of the paragraph and the first list than there is between blocks
- The last item in the list will either be followed by the rest of the paragraph that the list is part of or by a new paragraph. If the list is followed by a new paragraph, the list is followed by the standard space between blocks; if the list is followed by the rest of the paragraph that it is part of, there is less space than there is between blocks

Conclusion

Or, The real shortest chapter

You probably don't need to write a conclusion. It's a very unusual reader of a user manual that will read a conclusion.

22

More

Or, Shameless marketing

If liked this, you can get more. I blog on language and technical writing topics at http://rtfmphvis.blogspot.com; I also tweet (primarily on language usage as I run across it)—you can find me under the name phvogel or search on the hashmark #rtfm*.

About the author:

Peter Vogel has been writing user manuals and working with software developers for over 25 years. He also wrote the Technical write course for Learning Tree International which is taught around the world and has been translated into both Swedish and French. Peter has presented frequently for the Society for Technical Communication. You can contact Peter at peter.vogel@phvis.com.

www.ingramcontent.com/pod-product-compliance
Lightning Source LLC
Chambersburg PA
CBHW062104270326
41931CB00013B/3201